Rangers, Jayhawkers, and Bushwhackers in the Civil War

Untold History of the Civil War

CHELSEA HOUSE PUBLISHERS

Untold History of the Civil War

Rangers, Jayhawkers, and Bushwhackers in the Civil War

Douglas J. Savage

CHELSEA HOUSE PUBLISHERS
Philadelphia

Produced by Combined Publishing
P.O. Box 307, Conshohocken, Pennsylvania 19428
1-800-418-6065
E-mail:combined@combinedpublishing.com
web:www.combinedpublishing.com

CHELSEA HOUSE PUBLISHERS

Editor in Chief: Stephen Reginald
Managing Editor: James D. Gallagher
Production Manager: Pamela Loos
Art Director: Sara Davis
Director of Photography: Judy L. Hasday
Senior Production Editor: LeeAnne Gelletly
Assistant Editor: Anne Hill

Front Cover Illustration: "Confederate Sharpshooters" (c.1862) by William D.
Washington. Courtesy of the Museum of the Confederacy, Richmond, Virginia.

The Chelsea House World Wide Web site address is
http://www.chelseahouse.com

First Printing

135798642

Library of Congress Cataloging-in-Publication Data applied for:
ISBN 0-7910-5430-6

Contents

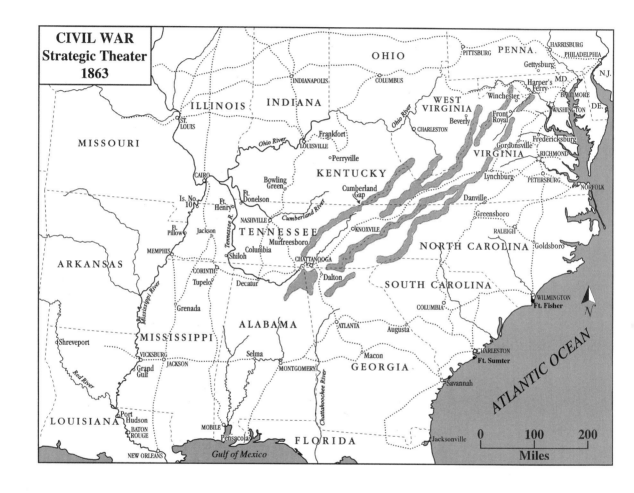

CIVIL WAR
Strategic Theater
1863

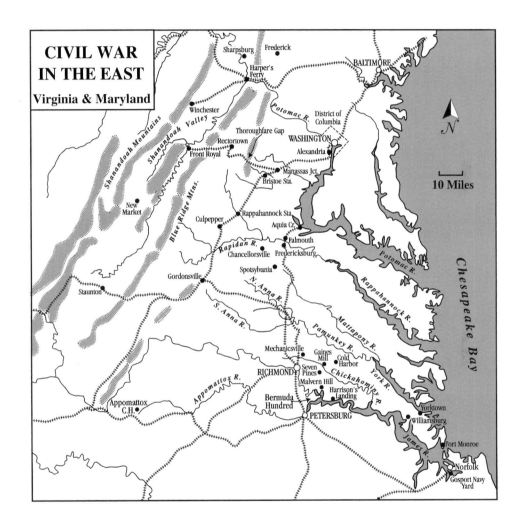

CIVIL WAR IN THE EAST
Virginia & Maryland

Sharpsburg
Frederick
Harper's Ferry
BALTIMORE
Winchester
Potomac R.
District of Columbia
Thoroughfare Gap
WASHINGTON
Rectortown
Front Royal
Alexandria
Shanandoah Mountains
Shanandoah Valley
Manassas Jct.
Bristoe Sta.
New Market
Blue Ridge Mtns.
Rappahannock Sta.
Culpepper
Aquia Cr.
Rapidan R.
Falmouth
Chancellorsville
Fredericksburg
Potomac R.
Spotsylvania
Gordonsville
N. Anna R.
Staunton
S. Anna R.
Rappahannock R.
Chesapeake Bay
Pamunkey R.
Mattapony R.
Mechanicsville
Gaines Mill
Cold Harbor
York R.
RICHMOND
Seven Pines
Chickahominy R.
Malvern Hill
Appomattox R.
Harrison's Landing
Bermuda Hundred
Yorktown
Appomattox C.H.
PETERSBURG
Williamsburg
James R.
Fort Monroe
Norfolk
Gosport Navy Yard

10 Miles

N

7

Civil War Chronology

1860

November 6 — Abraham Lincoln is elected president of the United States.

December 20 — South Carolina becomes the first state to secede from the Union.

1861

January-April — Mississippi, Florida, Alabama, Georgia, Louisiana, and Texas also secede from the Union.

April 1 — Bombardment of Fort Sumter begins the Civil War.

April-May — Lincoln calls for volunteers to fight the Southern rebellion, causing a second wave of secession with Virginia, Arkansas, Tennessee, and North Carolina all leaving the Union.

May — Union naval forces begin blockading the Confederate coast and reoccupying some Southern ports and offshore islands.

July 21 — Union forces are defeated at the battle of First Bull Run and withdraw to Washington.

1862

February — Previously unknown Union general Ulysses S. Grant captures Confederate garrisons in Tennessee at Fort Henry (February 6) and Fort Donelson (February 16).

March 7-8 — Confederates and their Cherokee allies are defeated at Pea Ridge, Arkansas.

March 8-9 — Naval battle at Hampton Roads, Virginia, involving the USS *Monitor* and the CSS *Virginia* (formerly the USS *Merrimac*) begins the era of the armored fighting ship.

April-July — The Union army marches on Richmond after an amphibious landing. Confederate forces block Northern advance in a series of battles. Robert E. Lee is placed in command of the main Confederate army in Virginia.

April 6-7 — Grant defeats the Southern army at Shiloh Church, Tennessee, after a costly two-day battle.

April 27 — New Orleans is captured by Union naval forces under Admiral David Farragut.

May 31 — The battle of Seven Pines (also called Fair Oaks) is fought and the Union lines are held.

August 29-30 — Lee wins substantial victory over the Army of the Potomac at the battle of Second Bull Run near Manassas, Virginia.

September 17 — Union General George B. McClellan repulses Lee's first invasion of the North at Antietam Creek near Sharpsburg, Maryland, in the bloodiest single day of the war.

November 13 — Grant begins operations against the key Confederate fortress at Vicksburg, Mississippi.

December 13 — Union forces suffer heavy losses storming Confederate positions at Fredericksburg, Virginia.

1863

January 1 — President Lincoln issues the Emancipation Proclamation, freeing the slaves in the Southern states.

May 1-6	Lee wins an impressive victory at Chancellorsville, but key Southern commander Thomas J. "Stonewall" Jackson dies of wounds, an irreplaceable loss for the Army of Northern Virginia.
June	The city of Vicksburg and the town of Port Hudson are held under siege by the Union army. They surrender on July 4.
July 1-3	Lee's second invasion of the North is decisively defeated at Gettysburg, Pennsylvania.
July 16	Union forces led by the black 54th Massachusetts Infantry attempt to regain control of Fort Sumter by attacking the Fort Wagner outpost.
September 19-20	Confederate victory at Chickamauga, Georgia, gives some hope to the South after disasters at Gettysburg and Vicksburg.

1864

February 17	A new Confederate submarine, the *Hunley,* attacks and sinks the USS *Housatonic* in the waters off Charleston.
March 9	General Grant is made supreme Union commander. He decides to campaign in the East with the Army of the Potomac while General William T. Sherman carries out a destructive march across the South from the Mississippi to the Atlantic coast.
May-June	In a series of costly battles (Wilderness, Spotsylvania, and Cold Harbor), Grant gradually encircles Lee's troops in the town of Petersburg, Richmond's railway link to the rest of the South.
June 19	The siege of Petersburg begins, lasting for nearly a year until the end of the war.
August 27	General Sherman captures Atlanta and begins the "March to the Sea," a campaign of destruction across Georgia and South Carolina.
November 8	Abraham Lincoln wins reelection, ending hope of the South getting a negotiated settlement.
November 30	Confederate forces are defeated at Franklin, Tennessee, losing five generals. Nashville is soon captured (December 15-16).

1865

April 2	Major Petersburg fortifications fall to the Union, making further resistance by Richmond impossible.
April 3-8	Lee withdraws his army from Richmond and attempts to reach Confederate forces still holding out in North Carolina. Union armies under Grant and Sheridan gradually encircle him.
April 9	Lee surrenders to Grant at Appomattox, Virginia, effectively ending the war.
April 14	Abraham Lincoln is assassinated by John Wilkes Booth, a Southern sympathizer.

Union Army
Army of the Potomac
Army of the James
Army of the Cumberland

Confederate Army
Army of Northern Virginia
Army of Tennessee

Harper's Weekly *featured a number of sketches like this one during the Civil War,* *depicting western towns being raided by out-of-control Rebel guerrillas.*

I

The Uncivil War

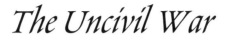

"Guerrillas," Union General William Tecumseh Sherman said on April 11, 1864, "are not soldiers, but wild beasts."

During the American Civil War, the vast majority of soldiers in Northern and Southern services were part of regular armies. They wore regulation uniforms, their governments issued to them the weapons they carried and the food they ate. They marched together and fought together, often in combat formations containing tens of thousands of men. At least three million men served in the armies and navies of the United States and the Confederate States. Of them, only about 10,000 served in so-called "irregular" military units which operated fairly independent of the regular armies and their regularly commissioned officers. These independent commands all may be called "irregulars," which simply means independent forces who fought where and when they chose, rather than under operating orders from regular army headquarters.

During the Civil War, these 10,000 irregular fighters called themselves by different names. Some were bushwhackers, some jayhawkers, some guerrillas, and most called themselves rangers. Each name carried a definite military or political meaning in the Civil War during 1861 through 1865. Generally, the first distinction can be made between guerrillas and rangers. Ranger units where usually mounted cavalry battalions which had some formal contact with regular armies. Often, ranger units took direct orders from regular officers in the army and sent official reports of their activities back to those regular army officers. Also, rangers tended to wear regulation army uniforms and that clothing clearly identified them with one side or the other.

Guerrilla fighters were very independent of regular army officers. They rarely reported to any higher officers and they often wore civilian clothing or even disguised themselves by wearing the uniforms of the enemies they were fighting.

During the Civil War, there were far more Confederate guerrilla and ranger forces than Union irregulars. It has been estimated that the South had at least 142 ranger battalions and 92 guerrilla bands. Most of the guerrilla units fought in the West, especially in Missouri, Kansas, and Arkansas.

The very nature of the Civil War required that the South should have the majority of these irregular fighting units. The Confederacy fought a "defensive" war: Southerners were defending their vast country from invading Federal armies. Fighting an "offensive" war, the North had to send armies into the South. This required long lines of communications to supply food, weapons, ammunition, medical supplies, and transportation to the Union forces entering the Confederacy. The Federal armies were far from their supply bases in the North. Only roads and railroads supplied them as they spent four bloody years crushing the Southern rebellion— what Southerners called their "War for Southern Independence."

Guerrilla and ranger forces were small units, often groups of only 10 soldiers, and rarely more than 100. While regular armies had between 60,000 and 150,000 men marching and fighting together, these small bands of mounted guerrillas and rangers could strike the Yankees' long wagon trains of supplies, or destroy railroads with lightning-fast raids. The largest guerrilla force in

Bushwhackers and jayhawkers usually were independent of the regular army and did not wear uniforms denoting which side they were on.

a single Civil War battle was only 450 cavalrymen. By way of comparison, at Gettysburg, Pennsylvania, in July 1863, General Robert E. Lee's Confederate army numbered 77,500 and General George Gordon Meade's Union army numbered 93,500 men. Fifty thousand men were killed, wounded, captured, or missing after three days of fighting.

A Rebel guerrilla band of 100 men could destroy miles of railroads or telegraph wires and be gone before the enemy even knew that they had been attacked. In all wars, guerrilla warfare best serves the side which is defending their own homeland. They know the hiding places and the smallest roads and pathways through the countryside. Small, hard-fighting units of guerrillas or rangers could slow or even reverse the progress of tens of thousands of regular troops.

The state of Missouri was a slave state which remained part of the non-slave North during the Civil War. The Civil War's most vicious and bloodiest guerrilla activities occurred in pro-Union Missouri and in the Confederate state of Kansas. In Missouri and Kansas, both Confederate and Union guerrilla bands slaughtered each other and came close to proving General Sherman's opinion that they were little more than "wild beasts." Roving bands of pro-slavery, anti-Union guerrilla units called themselves bushwhackers, and antislavery, pro-Union guerrilla bands called

One of General Ben McCullough's Texas Rangers.

themselves jayhawkers. Late in the war, as Confederate armies disintegrated, armed groups of deserters and draft-evaders from Confederate armies, especially in Louisiana and Florida, called themselves jayhawkers, although usually that name referred to men opposed to slavery and loyal to the Union. Generally, the real Confederate rangers fought in the East and the real guerrillas—at least the most vicious and bloodthirsty of the Rebel guerrillas—fought in the West. The terms bushwhackers and jayhawkers were also generally western terms.

In the Confederacy, the term "ranger" was given more legitimacy than "guerrilla" in April 1862 when the Confederate

Congress passed the Partisan Ranger Act. The act authorized the creation of independent battalions of rangers. The Congress in Richmond hoped that giving them official recognition would force the Yankees to treat captured rangers as prisoners of war, instead of guerrillas who could legally be executed when captured. The Partisan Ranger Act tried to link rangers to the national government and to regular fighting forces by declaring that "Such partisan rangers, after being regularly received in the service, shall be entitled to the same pay, rations, and quarters during their term of service and be subject to the same regulations as other soldiers." Three months later, on July 17, 1862, in Arkansas, Confederate General Thomas Hindman issued his own partisan ranger order which applied to any group of Rebel guerrillas numbering 10 or more. General Hindman ordered that "These companies will be governed in all respects by the same regulations as other troops."

Unfortunately, many rangers in the West were really little more than organized bands of murderers and looters, and were treated as such by the Federals who captured and executed many. In the East, especially in Virginia, partisan rangers did generally conform to regular army regulations and rules of warfare. These units were usually given prisoner-of-war legal status and were not executed as guerrillas. But there were gruesome exceptions.

These very real distinctions between loosely organized and very independent guerrillas and more disciplined, more military, less independent partisans or rangers can make it difficult to determine which of these units should be included in a history of Civil War guerrillas and rangers.

In Harper's Weekly *in 1861, these men were called irregular riflemen in the secessionist army.*

II

Regulars or Irregulars

Since the Confederate States of America fought a defensive war against invading armies from the North, they relied upon guerrilla and ranger warfare much more than did the Federals.

Some conventional cavalry units were thought of as cutthroat guerrillas by their enemies when they were really legitimate, regular cavalry units which bravely earned reputations for ferocious fighting. Most cavalry regiments and divisions were quite conventional—remaining close to the divisions of infantry "foot soldiers" to which they were assigned. The cavalry's assignment was to shadow their infantry divisions—to ride well ahead to scout for enemy infantry, and to patrol the flanks of large masses of infantry to prevent enemy attacks from the side or from behind. A few regular cavalry regiments distinguished themselves as "raiders" which specialized in hit-and-run attacks against enemy supply lines, wagon trains, railroads, and telegraph lines. Such raiders might have been hated by the enemy troops they harassed, cut off from food and ammunition, and isolated from communica-

John Morgan and his men are pictured here attacking a small town in Kentucky.

tions, but that did not make them irregulars in the technical sense.

An example of cavalry raiders who were not guerrillas or rangers would be the Confederate cavalry of Nathan Bedford Forrest. The Tennessee native entered Confederate service as a private and ended the war as a lieutenant general of cavalry. His raids against Union troops and communications extended through Tennessee and Mississippi. A ferocious fighter, Forrest was nearly stabbed to death in June 1863 by one of his own men. Forrest shot him dead. Forrest is credited with declaring the great military maxim, "Get there first with the most men." Usually, he did. But he commanded few independent operations compared to guerrillas or partisan rangers, and he usually fought in close association with other cavalry commanders and infantry army commanders. The Yankees might have thought that General Forrest was a ruthless ranger, but he was really a conventional cavalryman with unusual courage. After the war, his worst enemy, Yankee General William Tecumseh Sherman, said of Nathan Forrest, "I think Forrest was the most remarkable man our Civil War produced on either side."

Confederate cavalry leader John Hunt Morgan came closer to independent command and ranger operations. But he, too, was conventional cavalry under the command of regular army superiors. At the beginning of the war, he did raise an independent, volunteer unit of Kentucky soldiers loyal to the Confederacy, although Kentucky stayed in the Union. But even then, Morgan's unit was under the immediate command of regular Confederate Army General Simon Buckner. Operating somewhat independently as a Confederate colonel, John Hunt Morgan led a daring cavalry raid of 1,000 horsemen behind Yankee lines in the spring of 1862. He captured 17 towns and 1,200 Federal troops. Morgan even used one of the Civil War's first handheld batteries to create his own portable telegraph. He cut Yankee telegraph wires, spliced in his own telegraph, and sent messages to Federal telegraph stations with orders to hunt for Morgan's cavalry in all the wrong places. He became a brigadier general in regular Confederate service in December 1862. He was captured by the Federals in July 1863 after another amazing raid through Indiana, Kentucky, and southern Ohio. With penknives

John Hunt Morgan led his men on many daring missions for the Confederate army.

and table forks, he tunneled out of the Ohio Penitentiary in Columbus by November. He was killed in action in September 1864 in Tennessee. Morgan's enemies might have thought him a partisan ranger, but he was always regular Confederate cavalry, reporting his exploits and adventures to superior officers. Though a daring raider and soldier, he was technically neither a guerrilla nor a ranger.

Confederate Brigadier General John Daniel Imboden is also difficult to classify as irregular or regular army. He did command a cavalry unit called the 1st Virginia Partisan Rangers and he did occasionally conduct independent cavalry raids. But most of his Civil War career was spent fighting in support of regular Confederate infantry. He served early in the war with General Thomas "Stonewall" Jackson. After Stonewall's death in May 1863, General Imboden's cavalry rode with Robert E. Lee to Gettysburg. Then he commanded the Rebel cavalry of Lieutenant General Jubal Early's Confederate infantry. Typhoid fever took General Imboden out of active fighting for the last nine months of the war. General Imboden's Civil War career is a good example of the fact that calling a unit "partisan rangers" does not really make it an irregular unit.

Virginian Captain John Hanson McNeill did come closer to fitting the technical definition of a Confederate partisan ranger. He led the 18th Virginia Cavalry, known as "McNeill's Rangers," which

John McNeill led a band of men called McNeill's Rangers, who sometimes rode with John Mosby and his men.

General John D. Imboden commanded a cavalry unit called the 1st Virginia Partisan Rangers.

generally operated independent of higher command in Virginia and West Virginia. Captain McNeill's son was a lieutenant in his father's cavalry regiment.

McNeill's Rangers rode with the real ranger, John Singleton Mosby, in Mosby's raids through Virginia. In 1864, McNeill outraged regular Confederate officers by welcoming men who had deserted from regular Confederate armies into his rangers. He was court-martialed and acquitted for accepting deserters. In October 1864, McNeill was gravely wounded in the Shenandoah Valley of Virginia and died of his wounds in November.

Captain Harry Gilmor from Maryland led the 12th Virginia Cavalry and was also a ranger who may have crossed the line to guerrilla warfare at least once. Like John McNeill, Captain Gilmor often rode with John Mosby through Virginia, engaging in lightning raids against Federal infantry and supply lines. But his regiment also saw service as regular cavalry attached to Robert E. Lee's command at Gettysburg. After Gettysburg, his operations became more like guerrilla raids. His cavalry robbed Federal trains and even used the guerrilla tactic of dressing in Yankee uniforms to get closer to Federal forces. Gilmor was court-martialed and acquitted for robbing and abusing civilians in his train raids. In June 1864, he participated in burning the town of Chambersburg, Pennsylvania, near Gettysburg. He was captured and imprisoned twice during the Civil War and ended the war in a Yankee prison.

Among the more unusual guerrilla raids during the Civil War was the northernmost action of the entire war: the Rebel raid on St. Albans, Vermont, near the Canadian border. On October 19, 1864, Rebel Lieutenant Bennett H. Young and half a dozen Confederate loyalists robbed three banks in St. Albans in the name of the Confederacy. Riding stolen horses, they escaped to Canada with 200,000 Yankee dollars. Canadian authorities captured the guerrillas and returned the loot to Vermont. But Canada kept Lieutenant Young and his men as prisoners of war.

Although most Civil War ranger and guerrilla units were Confederate, the Union did have its share of independent units, generally cavalry, which spread terror through Confederate or pro-slavery Union states, especially in the West. The pro-Union, anti-slavery jayhawkers in Missouri and Kansas were the most notorious and vicious.

Confederate Harry Gilmor sometimes led his men using guerrilla-warfare tactics.

"Doc" Jennison and his Missouri jayhawkers were probably technically rangers although they behaved like guerrillas. Charles R. "Doc" Jennison was born in New York but moved to Kansas in 1857. A staunch antislavery man, Jennison organized the 7th Kansas Volunteer Cavalry when Civil War erupted in 1861. He proudly called his regiment Jennison's Jayhawkers. For more than a month during November and December 1861, Jennison's Jayhawkers robbed and looted Independence, Missouri. They murdered at least two civilians, including one man for the crime of not giving the 7th Kansas Volunteers liquor on demand.

Doc Jennison's second-in-command was Daniel R. Anthony—brother of women's rights advocate, Susan B. Anthony. From December 20, 1861, to January 8, 1862, Daniel Anthony led 250 of Jennison's Jayhawkers through Missouri, terrorizing the countryside. His men stole horses, freed slaves, and burned the towns of Columbus and Dayton, Missouri. The son of rabid abolitionist John Brown, who was hanged before the war for inciting slave uprisings, also served in Jennison's Jayhawkers. Since the atrocities committed by Jennison's irregulars were all done in the name of the Union, Federal General Henry Halleck wrote to Federal General George McClellan in December 1861 that "Jennison has done more for the enemy in this state than could have been accomplished by 20,000 of his own [Confederate] army." General Halleck was referring to the tremendous number of pro-Union, antislavery civilians in Missouri who were driven to support the Confederacy because of Doc Jennison's near-guerrilla behavior in Union blue.

By January 1862, Yankee General Henry Halleck in the West was condemning Jennison's Jayhawkers as "no better than a band of robbers," even though Jennison's Jayhawkers were Yankees determined to destroy Rebel property. General Halleck knew this when he said of Doc Jennison's men, "They disgrace the name and uniform of American soldiers." Jennison's men also executed unarmed and helpless Confederate prisoners.

Doc Jennison was finally relieved of command of the 7th Kansas Cavalry in the spring of 1862 due to his outrageous behavior. But within a year, he was returned to command with the rank of a Yankee colonel, this time in command of the 15th Kansas

Cavalry. In August 1863, Federal General Thomas Ewing issued an infamous order clearing civilians out of Jackson, Cass, Bates, and Vernon counties in Missouri so civilians loyal to the South could no longer help Rebel guerrilla bands in the area. Helping to force often innocent women and children from their Missouri farms and homes, Doc Jennison was back in the saddle, robbing and murdering in the process.

A little-known, pro-Union guerrilla band in Confederate Tennessee was led by Dave Beattie. The reputation of his battalion was such that Confederate General Braxton Bragg hanged 16 of Beattie's men as criminals.

Even some regular Union regiments were known to have behaved more like Missouri guerrillas. Federal Colonel Ivan Turchin started the Civil War in command of the 19th Illinois Volunteer Infantry. He was leading a brigade by May 1862. When his Yankees captured Athens, Alabama, he gave his men permission to loot the town. He simply told his regular soldiers, "I shut my eyes for an hour." Colonel Turchin's Federal superiors were so appalled that they tried to throw him out of the army. After Turchin's court-martial, he was promoted to brigadier general with the support of Secretary of War Edwin Stanton.

Likewise, Federal Major General David Hunter did not hesitate to use terror against civilians. In May 1864, General Hunter burned his way through Virginia's Shenandoah Valley in an effort to stop civilian support to Confederate ranger John Mosby. General Hunter issued an order that, "For every train fired or soldier assassinated, the house and other property of every secession sympathizer residing within a circuit of five miles shall be destroyed by fire; and for all public property taken or destroyed [by Confederate sympathizers] an assessment of five

Major General David Hunter was a Union leader who used guerrilla tactics, spreading terror in the civilian population.

times the value of such property will be made upon secession sympathizers residing within a circuit of ten miles."

When Federal General William Tecumseh Sherman was leading his army through Georgia in 1864 during Sherman's famous March to the Sea, reports reached General Sherman that Rebel guerrillas in Georgia were killing Union soldiers who were prisoners of war and mutilating their dead bodies. On November 30, 1864, General Sherman wrote to a Federal cavalry brigadier general, Hugh Kilpatrick: "[W]hen our men are found and you are full convinced the enemy have killed them after surrender in fair battle, or have mutilated their bodies . . . you may hang and mutilate man for man without regard to rank."

Allowing his own regular army units to act like undisciplined guerrillas, General Sherman so hated Rebel guerrilla fighters that he did not hesitate to use their tactics of terror against civilians in the South who helped guerrilla bands. On June 21, 1864, Sherman wrote to Secretary of War Stanton that "there is a class of people, men, women, and children, who must be killed or banished before we can hope for peace."

The military value of guerrilla and ranger regiments was significant. A handful of skilled guerrilla units could frustrate an entire army. As Federal Brigadier General Robert H. Milroy wrote in October 1862 in West Virginia, "We have now over 40,000 men in the service of the U.S. in West V[irginia] . . . [But] our large armies are useless here. They cannot catch guerrillas in the mountains any more than a cow can catch fleas."

But in spite of the occasional military successes of guerrilla bands and ranger units, especially Confederate units, even the Confederacy saw that guerrillas and rangers were bad for Southern morale and even worse for regular Confederate armies. In the South, so many regular soldiers deserted Confederate armies to join guerrilla bands and rangers that Confederate General Thomas L. Rosser wrote on January 11, 1864, "The effect on the service is bad." He argued that regular, well-disciplined soldiers resented the freedom enjoyed by roving bands of guerrillas and rangers which often were able to live in private homes when they were hiding from Federal armies. General Robert E. Lee agreed and he wrote on April 1, 1864, "I hope the order will be issued at once disbanding the companies and battalions [of guerrillas and rangers]."

Before the Civil War ended, the Confederacy did repeal its Partisan Ranger Act. But it was canceled too late. The terror and ferocity of guerrilla warfare had

NATHAN BEDFORD FORREST

Famed Confederate cavalryman Lieutenant General Nathan Bedford Forrest was born in Bedford County, Tennessee, in 1821. By the time the Civil War came, he was a successful farmer and slave trader. As a cavalryman specializing in raiding operations against Federal supply and communications lines, Forrest was feared, hated, and grudgingly respected by his Yankee enemies. His life and career were twice tainted by his racism. First, his name bears the stain of the Fort Pillow Massacre at Fort Pillow, Tennessee, 40 miles north of Memphis, which occurred during the Civil War on April 12, 1864. His force of 1,500 troopers stormed the fort defended by only 500 Federals—295 white infantry and 262 blacks of the United States Colored Troops. Overrun and hopelessly outnumbered, the Yankees surrendered. Forrest's men then slaughtered the white Yankees for fighting beside blacks, and the blacks just for being black.

After the war, the Ku Klux Klan was founded in Tennessee in 1866. The Klan was formed to fight the Reconstruction programs passed by the Federal Congress. Most white Southerners felt oppressed by Reconstruction legislation which made the Old South a military colony of the victorious North for 12 years. In 1867, the Klan held a convention in Nashville with delegates from other former Confederate states. Nathan Bedford Forrest was elected the national leader, the Grand Wizard of the Klan. As University of Chicago Professor John Hope Franklin noted in 1961, "They had one aim in common: . . . white supremacy in the South. They had one means in common: any and every kind of intimidation and violence against the Negro and his supporters." When Klan violence

Nathan Bedford Forrest

against blacks became too much even for Forrest, he resigned from the Klan in 1869. Two years later, Congress outlawed the Klan, but the KKK still exists and thrives in both North and South more than 125 years later. Considered a brilliant general for the South in the Civil War, the name of Nathan Bedford Forrest has also remained part of Klan history and terror since his death in Memphis in 1877.

changed the character of the war, especially in the West. As Dr. Richard S. Brownlee, director of the Missouri State Historical Society in 1958, wrote: "Almost unique in the history of the Civil War, acting at wide variance with the conventional military tactics of the period, these colorful and savage partisan cavalrymen ranged the border from Missouri to Texas for four long, terrible years."

And no Confederate ranger was more colorful or more vicious than the psychopathic killer, William Clarke Quantrill.

Frank and Jesse James pose with another Confederate soldier. The soon-to-be notorious outlaws fought under William Quantrill during the Civil War.

III

William Clarke Quantrill and Bloody Bill Anderson

Writing in 1962, historian Albert Castel said of William Quantrill, "It was to become a name linked to the bloodiest deeds of the Civil War."

When the Civil War began in April 1861, Missouri was an important border state with an explosive combination of political passions. The majority of Missouri citizens remained pro-Union, anti-Confederacy for the entire war, but Missouri was also a slave state. Therefore, great numbers of Missouri men wore Confederate gray to defend slavery or to oppose the Union, and great numbers wore Union blue. The bloody conflict between citizens and neighbors was ferocious. Missouri bushwhackers fought for the South and Missouri jayhawkers fought for the North. And each armed group fought the other without mercy.

Since Kansas was a free state, bushwhackers and jayhawkers often crossed the Missouri-Kansas border to spread terror and carnage.

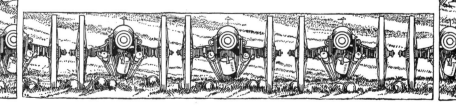

Missouri exploded four months into the war in August 1861. Federal commanding general for Missouri, John Frémont, issued an order freeing all Missouri slaves and seizing the private property of all Missouri citizens loyal to the South. Public outrage forced President Lincoln to cancel the general's order to keep pro-slavery Missouri in the Union. But the damage was already done. Pro-slavery bushwhackers and antislavery jayhawkers were soon cutting each other's throats in what historian Allan Nevins has called, "a vindictive and cruelly savage series of blows and retaliations."

Quantrill and his men are pictured here destroying the city of Lawrence, Kansas.

Confederate guerrillas went to work committing hit-and-run cavalry raids against Yankee supply depots, communications, transportation, and outposts across Kansas and Missouri. By December 1861, General Frémont had been replaced by General Henry Halleck. On December 22, General Halleck issued General Order Number 32 which ordered the death of all Rebel guerrillas and bushwhackers: "These men are guilty of the highest crime known to the code of war and the punishment is death. Anyone caught in the act will be immediately shot."

William Clarke Quantrill would soon become the name most feared and hated by the Federals, and most admired by western Confederates. An unlikely Rebel, young Quantrill was born in Canal Dover, Ohio. He never lived in the South before the Civil War. Three years before the war began, he had moved to Kansas. In December 1861, 24-year-old Quantrill decided that he was a Rebel guerrilla and he organized a tiny group of only 10 horsemen to attack Federals in Missouri. From that small beginning, Quantrill's guerrilla force would make the largest guerrilla attack of the entire war.

Quantrill attracted other angry men and born killers to his group. His ceremony for accepting men into his guerrilla regiment was simple. New men only had to say yes to Quantrill's question, "Will you follow orders, be true to your fellows, and kill all those who serve and support the Union?"

Doc Jennison's Missouri jayhawkers were the most responsible for the formation of Quantrill's band of killers. When Jennison's Jayhawkers were looting Jackson County, Missouri, during December 1861 and January 1862, Quantrill's horsemen followed the jayhawkers to recover the horses and property stolen by Doc Jennison and his pro-Union looters. Quantrill also decided to avenge the burning of Columbus and Dayton, Missouri, done by Dan Anthony's jawhawkers who were part of Doc Jennison's gang. So on March 7, 1862, William Quantrill and 40 bushwhackers rode into Aubry, Kansas, which is now Stilwell, Kansas. Quantrill's men killed five unarmed civilians, looted the town, and set fire to one building. The bloodbath of Missouri guerrilla warfare had started.

The Federals in Missouri and Kansas declared that guerrillas like Quantrill were not real soldiers but criminals. On March 13, 1862, General Halleck declared that "All persons are hereby warned that if they join any guerrilla band, they will not, if captured, be treated as ordinary prisoners of war, but will be hung as robbers and murderers." William Quantrill read General Halleck's order. After March 20, Quantrill started killing Yankee prisoners in retaliation—although there were a few exceptions when Quantrill released prisoners.

Shortly after General Halleck's order, he was replaced by Brigadier General John Schofield as commander of Federal forces in Missouri. General Schofield issued his own anti-guerrilla decree as General Order Number 18 on May 29, 1862. Confederate guerrillas and rangers, said Schofield, "will be shot down upon the spot."

On August 11, 1862, William Quantrill's force attacked the town of Independence, Missouri, defended by 300 Yankees commanded by Lieutenant Colonel James Buel. Surrounded, the Federals refused to surrender until Quantrill promised that he would not murder Yankee prisoners. Thirty-seven Federals were already dead with 63 others wounded. Quantrill gave his word—and kept it—and Colonel Buel surrendered the town. None of the Federal prisoners were harmed.

As with many of the self-proclaimed guerrillas and rangers, it is sometimes difficult to really decide what these men were. Although his actions were almost always completely independent of the Confederate government and rarely approved by Confederate army officers, it must be remembered that William Quantrill was, in fact, a Confederate army officer. By August 1862, Quantrill was a captain in the Confederate army.

On August 15, 1862, Quantrill's guerrillas formally mustered into the army of the Confederate States of America as semi-independent partisan rangers under the April 1862 Partisan Ranger Act. When the Confederate army's Colonel Gideon Thompson commissioned Quantrill a captain, it made it difficult for future historians to decide if Quantrill was a guerrilla or a more official ranger. There would be no doubt that Quantrill and his men were killers.

Within three weeks of becoming a Rebel captain, Quantrill and his band attacked Olathe, Kansas, on September 6, 1862. Quantrill captured the town, killing 12 civilian men. But he did not harm 125 Yankee prisoners of war whom he released after looting the town all night.

Continuing to make a name for his horsemen, Quantrill's force attacked Shawneetown, Kansas, on October 17, 1862. Quantrill now rode with 150 Rebel bushwhackers. Fifteen Union soldiers escorting a wagon train of supplies were killed. Ten Shawneetown civilians were also killed. Quantrill's men looted the town all night and then burned the entire village to the ground before riding back into Missouri.

As Quantrill's fame increased, so did the famous names among his men. Cole Younger joined the guerrillas after Yankees killed his father. Only 18 at the

Jesse James joined Quantrill's guerrilla band at the age of 17.

time, Cole Younger would become one of the West's most notorious gunslingers after the Civil War. Teenager Frank James joined in 1862. Two years later, his little brother, Jesse James, joined Quantrill. Some of Quantrill's men were barely teenagers. When jay-hawkers murdered the father of young Riley Crawford, Crawford's mother brought 14-year-old Riley to Quantrill herself. "Make him a soldier to kill Yankees," she said. Quantrill did and Riley was killed in action.

Quantrill and other Missouri guerrilla and ranger bands numbered only three to four thousand total. But during 1861 and 1862, they managed to keep

60,000 Yankees busy fighting them. Had the guerrillas not been in Missouri, these Federals could all have gone east to fight General Robert E. Lee in Virginia.

The Federals in the West desperately needed to clean out Confederate guerrillas and rangers. In May 1863, Yankee General Schofield divided Missouri and Kansas into two war zones, one commanded by General Thomas Ewing and one commanded by General James Blunt. General Ewing stirred Quantrill to new levels of bloodshed in August 1863.

On August 18, General Ewing issued his General Order Number 10, requiring the arrest of "all men and all women not heads of families who willfully aid and encourage guerrillas. . . . The wives and children of

Cole Younger was part of Quantrill's band before going on to becoming a notorious outlaw.

General John M. Schofield commanded Federal troops in Missouri. He issued a decree stating that Confederate guerrillas and rangers should be shot on sight.

known guerrillas, and also women who are heads of families and are willfully engaged in aiding guerrillas, will be notified . . . to remove out of this district and out of the State of Missouri forthwith." General Order Number 10 sent thousands of starving civilians barefoot onto dirt roads leading out of Missouri. Very quickly, William Clarke Quantrill and his men would become what Princeton University Professor James McPherson has called, "some of the most psychopathic killers in American history."

Quantrill set his sights on Lawrence, Kansas, a hotbed of pro-Union and jayhawker sentiment. Although some historians see Quantrill's Lawrence raid as a retaliation for General Ewing's infamous Order Number 10, historian Albert Castel argued in 1962 that Quantrill had been planning his attack on Lawrence before General Ewing issued his banishment order. Either way, Quantrill assembled 450 guerrillas in mid-August 1863. This was the largest guerrilla force of the Civil War.

Quantrill's Lawrence raid dripped with blood from the beginning. His men assembled in Johnson County, Missouri, during August 17 through 19. They crossed into Kansas on August 20. As they rode toward Lawrence, Quantrill needed local guides since his 450 horsemen traveled at night. During the night of August 20-21, Quantrill forced 10 Kansas farmers to lead the way, one at a time. As each farmer came to the end of country he knew, Quantrill's men murdered him and another local guide was pulled from his bed to lead the guerrillas toward Lawrence. All 10 guides were left dead between the Missouri border and Lawrence, Kansas.

As the sun came up on August 21, 1863, Quantrill's men were outside the city of 2,000 people. Quantrill gave his men simple orders: "Kill every man big enough to carry a gun."

On their way into Lawrence, Quantrill's 450 men surprised the 2nd United States Colored Troops infantry regiment and the 14th Cavalry. The guerrillas killed 17 of the Federals. By 7:00 in the morning, Quantrill rode into Lawrence. On the outskirts of town, Quantrill's little army rode under a black silk flag, the traditional symbol that no prisoners would be taken alive.

Union General Thomas Ewing tried to quell civilian support of Quantrill and his men.

Civilians were dragged from their beds and shot dead. Although no women were hurt or abused by Quantrill's guerrillas, at least 150 civilian, unarmed men were gunned down and killed. Another 30 men were wounded. Then Quantrill's men leveled the pro-Union town. They set fire to 185 stores and private homes. With Lawrence burning behind them, Quantrill and his men rode back to Missouri. One of Quantrill's men was captured by the people of Lawrence. They lynched him and dragged his dead body through town by the rope tied to his neck.

Four days later, General Ewing was hard at work writing another general order to crush civilian support in Missouri for Quantrill and other guerrilla bands. Ewing's new General Order Number 11 banished all Missouri citizens living

Union General James G. Blunt also served under General Schofield against the Southern guerrillas.

more than one mile from Federal outposts in Jackson, Cass, Bates, and Vernon counties. Everyone had to be out of their homes within 15 days, by September 9, 1863. Ten thousand civilians were forced to leave their homes and farms. The dreaded Doc Jennison and his jayhawker 15th Kansas Cavalry helped to evict civilians. Then he looted and burned their homes. By September 9, two-thirds of the civilians in three Missouri counties were gone. Historian Albert Castel called the banishment "the harshest military measure directed against civilians during the Civil War."

One month later, Quantrill tried to even the score. On October 6, Quantrill and 250 guerrillas put on Union blue uniforms as disguises—something legitimate Confederate "partisan rangers" would never do. Then they attacked a Union wagon train near Baxter Springs, Kansas. Among the Yankees in the wagons was General Blunt, one of the two district commanders of Federal forces in Kansas and Missouri. General Blunt escaped the ambush, but 79 Federal soldiers were killed, including a 12-year-old drummer boy. Among the dead was Major Henry Curtis, son of Federal Major General Samuel R. Curtis who had been in command of Federal troops in Missouri earlier in the war. Quantrill lost three guerrillas.

Not long after Baxter Springs, William Quantrill began losing control of his band of killers. By fall 1863, Quantrill took his guerrillas down to Texas. He received a mixed greeting from Confederate General

McCulloch. Writing to Lieutenant General Edward Kirby-Smith, Brigadier General Henry McCulloch said of Quantrill: "I appreciate his services and am anxious to have them; but certainly we cannot, as a Christian people, sanction a savage, inhuman warfare in which men are shot down like dogs after throwing down their arms and hold up their hands supplicating for mercy."

General McCulloch must have heard about Lawrence, Kansas.

By February 1864, General McCulloch had had enough of Quantrill and his rowdy killers. He wrote that "They regard the life of a man less than you would that of a sheep-killing dog."

Quantrill's command of bushwhackers all but disintegrated in Texas. Quantrill's most crazed guerrilla, William Anderson, known as Bloody Bill, had already left with many of Quantrill's own men for adventures of their own.

William Clark Quantrill took what was left of his command and rode north. He skirmished with Yankees for another 18 months, but his glory days were over. He led his remaining bushwhackers into Kentucky as the war was finally ending. One month after Robert E. Lee surrendered, Quantrill and his men fought in Spencer County, Kentucky. On May 10, 1865, Quantrill was badly wounded. Federals took him to a prison hospital at Louisville, Kentucky, where Quantrill died of his wounds on June 6, 1865. William Clarke Quantrill was only one month short of his 28th birthday.

Twenty-two years later, Quantrill's bones were taken from Kentucky and were reburied in his native Ohio.

SOME INFAMOUS MEMBERS OF QUANTRILL'S GUERRILLAS

FRANK AND JESSE JAMES

Frank James, older brother of Jesse James, rode with William Quantrill. Frank took part in Quantrill's Lawrence, Kansas, massacre and looting. Jesse James joined Quantrill in 1864 when he was only 17 years old. Frank and Jesse both left Quantrill's guerrillas to ride with the bloodthirsty Bloody Bill Anderson. When the Civil War ended, Frank joined brother Jesse and the Younger Brothers and went on a 10-year rampage of bank robberies. In 1868, the James and Younger brothers made off with $12,000 after a downtown gun battle in Russelville, Kentucky. When the four brothers robbed a bank in Gallatin, Missouri, in December 1869, they shot and killed a bank clerk. Eight days later, the James and Younger boys narrowly escaped an ambush by a sheriff's posse. In April 1872, the James brothers shot their way out of a bank in Columbia, Kentucky. At a bank in Northfield, Minnesota, in September 1876, another bank clerk was murdered. Making their escape, one of the gang was killed: Clell Miller— a veteran of Bloody Bill Anderson's guerrilla murderers of the Civil War. But the James boys escaped again. After the Minnesota gunfight, Frank and Jesse robbed trains together until Bob Ford murdered Jesse James in 1882. Bob Ford was living in Jesse James's home at St. Joseph's, Missouri, when he shot Jesse in the head while Jesse was hanging a picture on the wall. Frank James turned himself in to authorities in October 1882. He was never convicted of any of his crimes and went free in 1885. Frank lived quietly, stayed out of trouble for the next 30 years, and died a Missouri farmer in 1915.

JAMES AND COLE YOUNGER

James and Cole Younger had the same birthday, January 15, four years apart. Cole was born in 1844 and James in 1848. Both brothers rode with William Clark Quantrill during the Civil War where their criminal careers were joined with Frank and Jesse James. After the war, the Youngers robbed banks and murdered with the James boys. The Younger brothers joined Frank and Jesse in the 1868 bank robbery at Russellville, Kentucky, and a bank robbery in Columbia, Kentucky, in April 1872. A bank employee was killed in each robbery. Often joined by a third brother, Bob Younger, the Youngers robbed banks for another four years. In 1876, James, Cole, and Bob Younger joined the James brothers in the Northfield, Minnesota, bank robbery and shoot-out. The James brothers and Younger brothers escaped in different directions. Two weeks later, on September 21, a posse found the three Youngers. In a shootout, Cole Younger was shot eleven times, James was hit five times, and Bob was wounded three times. All three brothers lived to stand trial and

Cole Younger

Bob Younger (rear)

Jesse James

Frank James

The James Boys and the Younger Brothers

go to prison. Bob Younger died in 1889, after 13 years in prison. His two brothers spent 25 years in prison and were released in 1901. James Younger killed himself one year later. The last Younger brother, Cole, traveled the country in a Wild West show with Frank James. Cole died in 1916.

At least William Quantrill could claim to be a captain in the armies of the Confederate States of America. "Bloody Bill" Anderson may have joined Quantrill's guerrillas as a loyal Rebel, but he became little more than a vicious killer.

William Anderson grew up in Randolph County, Missouri, and Council Grove, Kansas—one a slave state; the other free. When Quantrill was losing control of his men in Texas in late 1863, Anderson left in December. Anderson's most loyal fellow guerrilla was teenager Archie Clement, only 18 in 1864. From Johnson City, Missouri, Clement was a butcher on the battlefield. He preferred to kill Yankees with his knife. Then he scalped the bodies when he had time.

If Bloody Bill Anderson was not yet an insane killer by August 1863, he became one on August 14. When General Ewing began arresting civilians, especially women, who were loyal to Rebel guerrillas in Missouri, Ewing arrested three sisters of William Anderson. The women were held in an old warehouse in Kansas City, Missouri. There is no doubt that Federal guards treated the women prisoners with kindness and cared for them as best they could. But the building was old and too crowded. On October 14, the prison building collapsed. One of Anderson's sisters was killed and the other two were hurt. Among the dead and injured women were cousins of Cole Younger and sisters of other Quantrill men.

The prison disaster turned William Anderson into "Bloody Bill." The director of the Missouri State Historical Society in 1958, Dr. Richard Brownlee, put it best: "Anderson became insane because of the injury to his sisters, and his attitude toward all men who supported or served the Union was that of a homicidal maniac." Historian Albert Castel added that Bloody Bill's "sole object was to kill as many Yankees as possible. And the more he killed, the more he wanted to kill."

There is no historical question that Bloody Bill was a guerrilla who operated completely independent of any Confederate control. He was not a partisan ranger reporting to Confederate superiors.

Bloody Bill satisfied his taste for Federal blood on September 27, 1864, at Centralia, Missouri. With 50 men who had formerly ridden with Quantrill, includ-

Archie Clement, Dave Pool, and Bill Hendricks fought under Quantrill. Clement became Bloody Bill Anderson's most loyal follower.

MORE INFAMOUS MEMBERS OF QUANTRILL'S GUERRILLAS

ROBERT WOODSON HITE

Sometimes known as Wood Hite, Robert Woodson Hite took part in Bloody Bill Anderson's murder and pillage in Missouri and Kansas. After the Civil War, Hite robbed a few trains with the help of his first cousins, Frank and Jesse James. Hite's first famous gunfight occurred in Kentucky in 1881. He shot and killed a man but bribed his way out of jail with $100. Leaving Kentucky, he went back to Missouri. In January 1882, Hite and Dick Liddell argued over the affections of a woman. Liddell had robbed trains with the James brothers. Hite and Liddell began firing their six-shooters at each other. Bob Ford was also there because the men were fighting over Ford's sister. Ford calmly ended the argument by shooting Robert Hite in the head. This was good practice for Bob Ford—four months later, Ford went down in history forever by shooting Jesse James in the head on April 3, 1882.

CLELLAND "CLELL" MILLER

Clell Miller rode with Bloody Bill Anderson's Rebel guerrillas during the Civil War. He became very close to Frank and Jesse James. After the war, he joined the James brothers and the Younger brothers in their crime sprees through the midwest. Miller was with the James brothers in April 1875 when they gunned down a Missouri farmer for hiding a detective whom the outlaws thought was on their trail. In September 1876, Miller joined the James and Younger brothers in a Northfield, Minnesota, bank robbery which turned into a running gunfight through Northfield streets. Clell Miller was shot and killed, but the James and Younger boys escaped.

OLIVER SHEPHERD

Shepherd learned bushwhacking from William Quantrill and Bloody Bill Anderson during the Civil War. After the war, he joined the James and Younger brothers in their robberies and murders. Shepherd, Frank and Jesse James, and Cole and James Younger committed the first daytime bank robbery in U.S. history when they robbed the Liberty, Missouri, bank in February 1866. Shepherd rode with the James and Younger brothers at the Russellville, Kentucky, bank robbery in March 1868 when the robbers had to fight a running gun battle to escape the town. In April 1868, Shepherd was cornered in Missouri by lawmen chasing him for the Kentucky bank robbery. Trying to shoot his way out, Shepherd was shot 20 times and died.

JIM REED

Jim Reed was 19 when he rode with William Clarke Quantrill's guerrillas during the Civil War. For the 10 years after the war, Reed lived a life of murder and robbery in Missouri, Texas, and Oklahoma. In 1873, he went to Oklahoma where he tortured a man until the helpless victim revealed where Reed could find $30,000 in U.S. government funds destined for the Creek Indian Nation. Six months later, Reed robbed a stage coach in Texas. Reed was shot and killed in August 1874 in Texas by his own friend—to collect a reward offered by authorities.

JIM CUMMINGS CLARK

Born in Missouri in 1841, Jim Clark rode with William Quantrill and became a close friend of the guerrilla leader. When the Civil War ended, Clark became a petty thief and boxer in Kentucky before moving to Colorado in 1887. The former Civil War guerrilla even became the town sheriff in Telluride, Colorado, until he was fired for beating criminals senseless with his bare hands. After he was fired, Clark threatened to kill any member of the Telluride City Council for 15 cents each. On August 6, 1895, Clark was shot and killed outside a Telluride saloon.

ing Frank and Jesse James, Anderson rode into Centralia to intercept a Yankee railroad train. The train from the East arrived at 11:30 in the morning. Bloody Bill's men pulled the passengers from the cars and lined them up in the fall sunshine. Twenty-four of the passengers were unarmed Federal soldiers on furlough from General William Tecumseh Sherman's army in Georgia. That was good enough for Bloody Bill. He executed all 24 helpless soldiers by shooting each man three times in the head. Archie Clement did most of the killing. Before the guerrillas rode out of town, they murdered two civilian passengers.

After the guerrillas rode out of Centralia, the 39th Missouri Militia of mounted infantry arrived at the train at 1:00 in the afternoon and saw the horror left by Bloody Bill. The horsemen rode hard in pursuit of Anderson's guerrillas.

The Union horsemen caught Bloody Bill three miles out of Centralia. Bloody Bill's 50 guerrillas attacked the 147 Federals and slaughtered 124 of them. Young Archie Clement particularly enjoyed himself by scalping the dead Yankees.

Standing over the mutilated bodies, Bloody Bill declared, "From this time forward, I ask no quarter and I give none."

Bloody Bill's rampage continued for another month. On October 26, 1864, Bloody Bill and 70 guerrillas were ambushed by 150 Federals near Albany, Missouri. The Yankee Missouri militia remembered the massacre of their comrades after the Centralia raid. Fighting ferociously, the Federals shot and killed William Anderson, not quite one year after he had left Quantrill's command.

IV

John Singleton Mosby and His Men

"*I*n war," John Singleton Mosby wrote after the Civil War, "a great deal must be left to chance."

Although his Yankee enemies called John Mosby a guerrilla and threatened to hang him if captured, Colonel Mosby fits all definitions of a partisan ranger: he held Confederate army rank and he always reported to superior officers in the regular Confederate army. Born in Virginia in 1833, he attended the University of Virginia. But he was thrown out of college after he shot another student. While in prison, he read law books and became a lawyer in Bristol, Virginia, before the Civil War.

Mosby entered Confederate service as a private. He served as a scout for the illustrious Rebel cavalryman, General James E. B. Stuart, known as Jeb. While serving Jeb Stuart, Mosby was captured and released in 1862. He was then promoted to captain and was authorized to form an independent cavalry command of partisan rangers. Throughout his Rebel career, Captain, then Colonel Mosby reported directly to Jeb

Colonel John Singleton Mosby led a band of partisan rangers for the Confederate army.

Stuart until General Stuart was killed in May 1864. After Stuart's death, Mosby often sent his written battlefield reports directly to Robert E. Lee. Mosby never met the total independence requirement of a true guerrilla battalion, and only very rarely did his actions degenerate into guerrilla-style murder.

Shortly after the Civil War, Confederate Lieutenant General Jubal Early said of Mosby's command: "Mosby's battalion, though called guerrillas by the enemy, was a regular organization in the Confederate Army, and was merely serving on detached duty under General Lee's orders."

James Williamson, a veteran of the ranger battalion known simply as "Mosby's Men," although officially Mosby's unit was the 43rd Virginia Cavalry, said of his battalion after the war: "They never masqueraded in the uniforms of Federals, except that through force of circumstances men at times wore blue overcoats captured by them from Federal cavalry. This was because they could get no others." Guerrilla bands like Quantrill's deliberately wore Union blue to disguise themselves, as Quantrill did at Baxter Springs.

The consensus of historians is that John Mosby was a Confederate partisan ranger under the Partisan Ranger Act of April 1862, and was neither a guerrilla nor a bushwhacker.

Mosby's rangers already had a reputation for courage and adventure by the spring of 1863. But they cemented that reputation forever among Confederates on March 8, 1863. Mosby and 29 handpicked rangers made their way well behind Yankee lines at Fairfax Court House, Virginia, between Centreville and Alexandria. John Mosby managed to get inside the headquarters building of Yankee Brigadier General Edwin H. Stoughton. Getting all the way to General Stoughton's bedroom, Mosby found the Yankee sleeping soundly. As John Mosby remembered years later:

> As the general was not awakened by the noise we made in entering the room, I walked up to his bed and pulled off the covering. But even this did not arouse him. . . . So I just pulled up his shirt and gave him a spank. . . . He had not realized that we were not some of his staff. I leaned over and said to him: "General, did you ever hear of Mosby?"

Mosby served under Confederate General Jeb Stuart until Stuart's death in May 1864.

51

"Yes," he quickly answered, "have you caught him?" "No," I said. "I'm Mosby—he has caught you."

Riding out of Fairfax with their high-ranking and mortified prisoner, Mosby also captured two Yankee captains, 30 privates, and 58 horses. Mosby released General Stoughton to Confederate General Fitzhugh Lee, Robert E. Lee's nephew. Stoughton and Fitzhugh had been classmates at West Point.

When Captain Mosby sent his official report of the adventure to Jeb Stuart, General Stuart sent the report on to Robert E. Lee. On March 27, 1863, Jeb Stuart sent Mosby a telegram in which Stuart said that General Lee's reaction to Mosby's report was "Hurrah for Mosby! I wish I had a hundred of him!"

As further reward for the Fairfax kidnapping of a Yankee general, Mosby was promoted to major on April 4, 1863.

Although Mosby's 43rd Virginia Cavalry mustered some 800 men, Major Mosby conducted most of his raids with small groups of rangers, often no more than 50, to better conduct fast hit-and-run attacks. Major Mosby's daring career nearly ended on June 22, 1863, in the Bull Run Mountains of Virginia. Forty Yankee cavalry and 100 infantrymen ambushed Mosby who had only 30 rangers at his side. Mosby escaped with two of his men wounded. Major General George Gordon Meade reported to his Federal superiors on the same day, "I came near catching our friend Mosby this morning." Five days later, General Meade was promoted and found himself marching into Pennsylvania to a place called Gettysburg.

The battle of Gettysburg ended on July 3, 1863, and Robert E. Lee began his retreat back to Virginia the next day. When General Meade's Federals followed and tried to destroy Lee's shattered army, Mosby was busy pecking at Meade's supply lines to slow the Yankee chase. By July 28, 1863, Mosby's rangers had captured 186 Federal prisoners, 123 horses and mules branded "US," and 12 wagons full of Federal supplies. On August 11, Mosby's Men captured another 19 Yankee supply wagons in Virginia.

On August 24, 1863, Mosby and only 35 of his rangers attacked the 2nd Massachusetts Cavalry, 10 miles from Alexandria, Virginia. Mosby captured 12 Yankee prisoners and 85 horses. But two rangers were killed and John Mosby was wounded in the leg—his first of seven wounds during the war.

By the middle of September, Major Mosby was back in the saddle. On October 27, 1863, he did what he did best. A huge Federal wagon train of supplies moved slowly near Warrenton, Virginia. Two full regiments of foot soldiers guarded the wagons of precious sup-

Mosby's Men are depicted attacking a large Union wagon train.

plies. Major Mosby and 50 rangers raided only the center of the wagon train, unhooked and captured 127 mules and 27 horses, and rode away without anyone firing a single shot.

By the end of 1863, Major Mosby's fame was so widespread in the South that regular soldiers in Confederate armies began deserting their regiments so they could romp in Mosby's rangers. To stop this dangerous trend, Major Mosby issued official certificates of ranger membership to his men on November 2, 1863, to separate his rangers from deserters. John Mosby signed each of the nearly 800 certificates.

By November 26, 1863, Mosby's Men were again stealing Yankee horses for the Confederate cavalries and mules for Rebel supply, artillery, and ambulance wagons. Near Brandy Station, Virginia, the Rebel rangers captured 160 mules and 7 horses. December raids captured 100 Yankee prisoners and 100 horses and mules.

But Federals certainly thought of Mosby's Men as guerrillas. On January 10, 1864, Mosby and 110 rangers attacked the Loudoun County, Virginia, camp of 200 Maryland cavalrymen. Four Federals were killed and 17 wounded. Mosby lost 8 rangers. Major Henry Cole of the Yankee cavalry in his official report of the attack described "an attempt by Major Mosby's battalion of guerrilla cavalry to surprise and capture my camp."

Whether guerrilla or ranger, Robert E. Lee recommended Mosby's promotion to lieutenant colonel on January 21, 1864.

On February 22, 1864, Mosby and 160 rangers engaged the 2nd Massachusetts Cavalry's 180 horsemen at Dranesville, Virginia. Colonel Mosby waited concealed within a pine forest for the Yankees to approach. He signaled the attack with a whistle.

Mosby and his men attacked Union supply wagons to replenish their own dwindling supplies.

Private Williamson remembered the moment 32 years later:

> There was an unnatural, and unearthly stillness around us at that moment—a stillness which seemed to creep over our flesh like a chill, and to be seen and felt; when suddenly, out of this ghostly silence, there came that shrill, warning signal, like the fierce, wild shriek of the wind rushing through the trees of the forest, giving warning of the coming storm.

In that storm, 15 Federal cavalrymen died, 25 were wounded, and 75 were captured along with 90 horses. Mosby's rangers had only one killed and five wounded.

When John Mosby submitted his formal, after-action report on February 23, General Jeb Stuart added his own personal endorsement before forwarding the report up the chain of command to Robert E. Lee: "This is another of the many brilliant exploits of this gallant leader." When the report reached General Lee, he endorsed the document, "Respectfully forwarded, united in the commendation bestowed by General Stuart." The report then went on to the desk of the Confederate secretary of war.

By July 5, 1864, Mosby tangled again with the 2nd Massachusetts Cavalry at Mount Zion, Virginia, near Leesburg. The Federal horsemen were reinforced by the 13th New York Cavalry. The Federals lost 17 killed, 40 wounded, and 57 men and 100 horses captured. The Rebel rangers lost seven wounded with no one killed.

Federals were growing quicker to brand Mosby's Men as guerrillas as 1864 dragged on. On August 13, Lieutenant Colonel Mosby led 330 rangers in an attack on a large Federal wagon train of supplies near Berryville in the Shenandoah Valley. The supplies were bound for Union General Phil Sheridan's camp near Winchester, Virginia. At the price of two rangers killed and three wounded, Mosby captured 500 mules, 36 horses, 200 head of cattle (to feed hungry Confederate soldiers), and 208 Yankee prisoners. The rangers burned 100 wagons.

Lieutenant General Ulysses S. Grant was fed up with Mosby's rangers. Three days after Berryville, General Grant wired Phil Sheridan, "Where any of Mosby's men are caught, hang them without trial."

Three days after Grant's telegram, Mosby's Men began an ugly blood feud with General George Armstrong Custer's Michigan cavalry. On August 19, Mosby's rangers attacked the 5th Michigan Cavalry near Berryville. Sixteen Federals were killed.

A month later, on September 15, Lieutenant Colonel Mosby was wounded again at Falls Church, Virginia. He and only two rangers had crossed the path of the 13th New York Cavalry.

While Colonel Mosby was recovering from his second wound, his rangers fought the 2nd United States Cavalry on September 23, near Front Royal, Virginia. Following General Grant's orders of August 16, Yankee General Wesley Merritt executed six captured rangers. Four were shot and two were hanged. General Merritt pinned a note on the back of one of the hanged rangers. It said, "Such is the fate of all of Mosby's men."

Colonel Mosby returned to duty in late September, after the execution of his men. On October 14, Mosby and

Union General Wesley Merritt executed six of Mosby's men after they were captured in Virginia.

84 rangers attacked a Federal railroad train in the Shenandoah Valley. They destroyed 10 cars and captured $168,000 of Yankee paper money. On the 29th, Mosby sent a formal letter to General Lee about the hanging of Mosby's men. Mosby asked Lee's permission to execute captured Yankees. "It is my purpose to hang an equal number of Custer's men whenever I capture them." Mosby held General Custer responsible for General Merritt's atrocity at Front Royal. General Merritt commanded the 1st Cavalry Division of General Phil Sheridan's army in the Shenandoah Valley. General Custer, the youngest general in the Union Army at age 24, commanded the 3rd U.S.

Cavalry in Sheridan's force. General Lee approved Mosby's execution request.

Wrong in blaming General Custer for the rangers' executions, Colonel Mosby captured 27 of Custer's cavalrymen on November 6, 1864. He had the helpless Federals draw lots to select seven to die. Five were executed and two escaped. John Mosby personally wrote the note pinned to one of the three Federal prisoners hanged: "These men have been hung in retaliation for an equal number of Colonel Mosby's men hung by orders of General Custer at Front Royal. Measure for measure."

The measure-for-measure murders stopped, but the fighting and dying continued for another six months. On December 21, 1864, Colonel Mosby was wounded again near Fauquier, Virginia, while he was having dinner in a private house. His doctor believed that the serious abdominal wound would be fatal. Mosby survived again, returning to duty in late February 1865.

The Civil War in Virginia ended April 9, 1865, when General Lee surrendered to General Grant. John Mosby refused to formally surrender his partisan rangers. On April 21, he simply disbanded his battalion and sent his survivors home. "I disband your organization," he announced, "in preference to surrendering it to our enemies." Two months later, John Singleton Mosby surrendered to Federal authorities alone.

With the holocaust of civil war over and 660,000 men dead in the North and South, John Mosby found himself becoming a friend of Ulysses S. Grant, the man who wanted Mosby to hang. Mosby supported Grant's campaign for the presidency in 1868 and again in 1872. Grant appointed his old Rebel enemy U.S. consul to Hong Kong.

Many Southerners never forgave John Mosby for becoming Grant's friend after the war.

During the last months of former President Grant's life in 1885, he wrote his memoirs. In his recollections, he remember John Singleton Mosby: "Since the close of the war, I have come to know Colonel Mosby personally, and somewhat intimately. . . . He is able and thoroughly honest and truthful. There were probably but few men in the South who could have commanded successfully a separate detachment in the rear of an opposing army, and so near the border of hostilities as long as he did, without losing his entire command."

Ten years after Grant's kind words for an old enemy, John Mosby attended the 30th Reunion of Mosby's Men at Alexandria, Virginia, on January 16, 1895. Colonel Mosby said to the old soldiers gathered around him: "Nearly thirty years have passed away, and we meet once more on the banks of the Potomac and in sight of the Capitol, not in hostile array, but as citizens of a great and united country."

Colonel Mosby, who had studied law in prison, went back to the law after the war. He became a lawyer in Warrenton, Virginia, and died there in 1916.

Glossary

abolitionists	People who worked for the abolishment of slavery.
bluecoats	Term used for soldiers in the Northern Union army during the Civil War because of the color of their uniforms.
bushwhackers	Pro-slavery, anti-Union guerrilla units.
cavalry	An army unit mounted on horseback.
Confederacy	The Confederate States of America; the South.
Confederate	Citizen of the Confederate States of America; a Southerner during the Civil War.
Federals	A name used for members of the Union.
graycoats	Term used for soldiers in the Southern Confederate army during the Civil War because of the color of their uniforms.
guerrilla	A person who engages in irregular warfare using sabotage, harassment, and often violent tactics.
irregulars	A soldier who is not a member of a regular military force but acts and fights on their own.
jayhawkers	Usually antislavery, pro-Union guerrilla bands; towards the end of the Civil War some Southern units used the name also.
Partisan Rangers Act	An act passed by the Confederate Congress in 1862 that allowed for the formation of independent battalions of rangers.
raiders	Soldiers who specialized in hit-and-run attacks on enemy supply lines and communication lines.

rangers	Mounted cavalry usually connected in some way with regular armies, who used irregular or guerrilla tactics.
Rebels	Term used for Southerners in the Civil War.
regulars	Soldiers in the official army.
secessionist	Southerners who voted to secede from the Union and form their own republic.
Union	The United States of America; the North.
War for Southern Independence	One of the names Southerners gave to the Civil War. Others were the War Between the States and War of the Rebellion.
Yankees	Term used for Northerners during the Civil War.

Further Reading

Brownlee, Richard S., *Gray Ghosts of the Confederacy: Guerrilla Warfare in the West, 1861-1865*. Baton Rouge: Louisiana State University Press, 1958.

Castel, Albert. *William Clarke Quantrill: His Life and Times*. New York: Frederick Fell, 1962.

Editors of Time-Life Books. *Spies, Scouts and Raiders*. Alexandria, VA: Time-Life Books, 1985.

Monaghan, Jay. *Civil War on the Western Border, 1854-1865*. New York: Bonanza Books, 1955.

Williamson, James J. *Mosby's Rangers*. New York: Ralph B. Kenyon, 1896.

Websites About Rangers, Jayhawkers, and Bushwhackers in the Civil War

Confederate Irregular Warfare 1861-1865:
    http://hem.passagen.se/csa01/index.html.

The James-Younger Gang:
    http://web.islandnet.com/~the-gang/

John Singleton Mosby:
    http://www.civilwarhome.com/mosbybio.htm

William "Bloody Bill" Anderson:
    http://www.calweb.com/~rbbusman/outlaws/
    anderson.html

William Clarke Quantrill:
    http://www3.pbs.org/weta/thewest/wpages/wpgs400/
    w4quantr.htm

Index

INDEX

PHOTO CREDITS
Bettmann/CORBIS: pp. 30, 36, 37; CORBIS: pp. 43, 45; *Harper's Weekly*: pp. 10,/ 13, 14, 16, 18, 19, 20, 26, 32, 38, 40, 50, 51, 53, 55; Library of Congress: pp. 21, 23, 39, 57